Classic Desserts Of Hungary

Delicious Hungarian Dessert Recipes That Are Worth To Try

Copyright © 2021

DEDICATION

Contents

Dobosh Torte

Ingredients

For the Cake:

8-ounces butter (unsalted, room temperature)

1 cup sugar

4 large eggs (room temperature, lightly beaten)

1 1/2 cups all-purpose flour

1 teaspoon vanilla extract

For the Filling:

8-ounces semisweet chocolate (chopped)

2-ounces unsweetened chocolate (chopped)

1 pound butter (unsalted, room temperature)

5 large egg whites (room temperature)

1 cup sugar

For the Caramel Glaze:

2/3 cup sugar

1/3 cup water

Garnish: ground nuts of choice (to sprinkle on top and sides of cake)

Steps to Make It

While there are multiple steps to this recipe, this seven-layer sponge cake is broken down into workable categories to help you better plan for preparation and baking.

Make the Cake

Gather the ingredients. Preheat oven to 350 F.

coating.

With a buttered knife, mark the glaze before it completely hardens into 16 equal wedges without cutting all the way through.

Assemble the Torte

Place 1 cake layer on a serving plate, or in a 9-inch springform pan to use as a guide, and spread on 1/8-inch of filling.

Repeat with remaining layers and portions of filling, and finish with the glazed layer on top.

Use the rest of the filling to cover the sides of the cake. Sprinkle with ground nuts of choice, if desired. Refrigerate until serving.

To serve, slice along the lines marked in the caramel glaze.

Krémes

Ingredients for 12 servings 40 min

VANILLA-INFUSED MILK

2 cups milk

1 vanilla bean

FLAKY PASTRY

1 ½ cup flour + 1 tbsp

3/4 cup margarine

1 pinch salt

4 tbsp cold water

4 tsp vinegar

CUSTARD

8 egg yolks

1/2 cup sugar

1/3 cup flour + 1 tbsp

2 packages (2 tbsp) vanilla sugar

3 packages (21 g) gelatine

1/4 cup unsalted butter

8 egg whites

1/2 cup sugar

1 tsp fresh lemon juice

FOR DUSTING

1/4 cup powdered sugar

Steps to Make It

Start by making the vanilla-infused milk. Place the milk in a small saucepan and heat it over low to medium heat. Take the vanilla bean, scrape the seeds into the milk, and toss the bean pod into the milk as well. Cover the saucepan, remove it from heat, and leave for 1 hour.

The next step is to prepare the flaky pastry. Place chilled margarine and flour into a large bowl and combine them into fine crumbs. Add salt, water, and vinegar, and knead into a firm dough.

Flour the working surface generously and roll out the dough into a thin rectangle. Divide it into 4 parts, then roll out each part and stack them on top of one another. Place in a refrigerator for 20 minutes.

Meanwhile, preheat the oven to 400°F.

Cut the chilled dough in half. Take the first half and roll it out very thinly - this will be the top of your krémes. Now, fold the dough in half and transfer it into a 9x13-inch baking pan. Unfold the dough and arrange it, so it goes halfway up the sides of a baking dish and so possible, cut in half, and pricked with a fork. The dough is usually baked in an oven preheated to 180°C until it becomes golden. The half which will end up on top of the krémes should be cut into equal-sized squares before being placed on the custard, which will make cutting significantly easier.

Vanilla

When it comes to custard, using a real vanilla bean instead of vanilla extract is what differentiates excellent krémes from the regular ones. Small black spots in the vanilla custard indicate that the krémes were made with vanilla beans. When choosing a vanilla bean, make sure it is plump, pliable, and that it has a strong vanilla scent. Best vanilla beans usually come from Madagascar, Mexico, and Indonesia, and should be stored in air-tight containers or zip-lock bags.

Eggs

The classic approach for making the krémes custard is to separate the egg whites from the egg yolks. The egg whites are then whipped with sugar into a firm snow, which is gently folded into the custard.

Thickening Agents

Flour and gelatin are the most common thickening agents for the custard. The flour will make the custard slightly denser and heavier, while the use of gelatin will make the custard wobblier and lighter.

Serving

Most commonly, krémes are dusted generously with powdered sugar before being served. Modern versions suggest glazing krémes with chocolate or placing a layer of whipped cream on top of the custard. Make sure you serve krémes cold, right out of the refrigerator.

Pogácsa

Ingredients

1/2 cup whole milk, heated to 110 degrees F to 115 degrees F

2 teaspoons active dry yeast

1/2 teaspoon sugar

4 cups all-purpose flour

5 ounces gruyere cheese, finely shredded

1 tablespoon salt

2 eggs

14 tablespoons unsalted butter, softened (1 3/4 American sticks)

1/2 cup sour cream

TOPPING

1 egg yolk

2 ounces gruyere cheese, finely shredded

Steps to Make It

In a large bowl, combine milk, yeast and sugar and let stand until yeast is softened, about 10 minutes.

Add flour, cheese, salt, eggs, butter, and sour cream to the yeast mixture. Using an electric mixer, mix on low speed until dough comes together. Beat on medium speed 1 to 2 minutes. The dough should be smooth and not sticky.

Roll dough 1/2 inch thick on a lightly floured surface. Make a shallow cross-hatched pattern with the point of a sharp knife over the top of the dough and brush with egg yolk. Sprinkle cheese on top, and cut out rounds with a 1 to 1 1/2 inch cutter.

Arrange circles in rows on a parchment-lined baking sheet, about 1/4 inch apart. Put pan in a cold oven and set temperature to 400 degrees F. Bake about 25 minutes, until pogacsa are nicely browned on their tops and bottoms. Let cool completely and store airtight.

Pogacsa may also be frozen up to 1 month. Thaw and reheat at 225 degrees F for 20 minutes.

Kakaós Csiga

Ingredients

Dough

600 grams Flour

30 grams Yeast

50 grams Sugar

100 ml Milk

200 ml Milk more if needed

2 Egg Yolks

2 tbsp Oil

1 tsp Sugar

Pinch of Salt

Filling

100 grams Butter melted

6 tbsp Unsweetened Cocoa Powder

100 grams Sugar

200 ml Sweetened Milk

Steps to Make It

In a small saucepan over a low-medium flame, heat 100ml of milk with a tsp of Sugar. When the milk is warm dissolve your yeast, using a wooden spoon.

In a mixing bowl, add in your dry ingredients: flour, egg yolks, salt and sugar. Make a well in the middle of the flour and gradually add in the milk-yeast mixture. Start kneading and adding the oil. If the dough is too dry add in more milk. Leave, covered for an hour or until it's doubled in side.

When the dough has risen, divide it into two. Roll out into a rectangle shape, do this for both batches.

In a bowl mix cocoa powder, melted butter and the sugar. Then spread this mixture onto the rolled-out dough.

Roll up the dough, similar to cinnamon roll and slice into smaller rolls. Place them in a baking dish and grease the tops with more melted butter.

Put them in a cold oven and bake them for about 20-25 minutes on 170c, gas mark 3.

10 minutes brush with sweetened milk.

Sprinkle powdered sugar on top then serve.

Palacsinta

Ingredients

1 egg

1 teaspoon of sugar

150 grams (5.4 ounces) of plain flour

300 ml (1 ¼ cups) of whole milk

150 ml of sparkling water or ½ coffee-spoon of baking soda + 150 ml water (2/3 cup)

Pinch of salt

Oil for frying (I use sunflower oil)

150 grams (2/3 cup) of dry cottage cheese (or ricotta or farmer's cheese)

1 egg yolk

1 heaping tablespoon of sugar

1 little splash of vanilla extract (or 1 sachet of vanilla sugar – around 1 flat tablespoon)

Zest of half a lemon

Apricot jam

Icing sugar for dusting

Takes 30 min

Makes 8-10 pancakes.

Steps to Make It

Break the egg, add a pinch of salt and one teaspoon of sugar and beat until smooth.

Add some milk and some flour and mix well. I always add the

ingredients gradually to avoid lumps.

When it is smooth, add the remaining flour, milk, and soda water. You can use sparkling water or still water with half a coffee-spoon baking soda.

The ideal pancake batter consistency is when the batter is not too runny and yet, not too stiff. It is like a thin yoghurt drink.

Put the pancake batter in the fridge for 5-10 minutes; meanwhile, make the sweet cottage cheese filling

Separate an egg, you need only the yolk for this recipe. Beat the yolk with the sugar and vanilla until thick.

Put the cottage cheese in a bowl. Mash the cheese very well until it becomes absolutely soft. Now add the egg yolk and sugar mixture and the zest from half a lemon. Mix all the ingredients very nicely until the mixture reaches a uniform consistency.

Fry the pancakes: Set a frying pan over medium heat. Add a few drops of vegetable oil. When it is hot, pour some pancake batter into the frying pan. Tilt the pan so that the batter coats the surface of the pan evenly. This should be a very thin coat. If you have holes, fill them with some batter. Always stir the mixture before pouring it into the hot pan, or the flour might settle. Fry the underside of the pancake for approximately 1 minute or until golden brown. You can loosen it with the spatula. Check the underside to be sure it has browned.

Flip the pancake to fry the topside as well. The pancake is done when both sides are a light brown.

Spread each pancake with jam or cottage cheese and roll up. Sprinkle with icing sugar. Serve immediately.

Zserbó

Ingredients

500 grams (17.6 ounces) of plain flour

250 grams (8.8 ounces) of margarine or butter

25 grams (0.9 ounces) of fresh yeast

1 whole egg

2 egg yolks

1 tablespoon of sugar

100 ml (0.44 cups) of whole milk

Zest of half a lemon

Pinch of salt

150 grams (5.3 ounces) of ground walnuts

50 grams (1.8 ounces) of powdered sugar

400 grams (14.1 ounces) of homemade apricot jam

100 grams (1 stick) of butter

4 tablespoons of sugar

4 tablespoons of cocoa powder (20-22%)

4 tablespoons of water

Takes 2 hours

Serves 8.

Steps to Make It

In a smaller pan heat milk until lukewarm and dissolve the sugar and the yeast.

In a large bowl mix the flour and the cubed 250g (8,8 ounces) margarine or butter by hand. The mixture will be quite crumbly.

Add the whole egg, 2 egg yolks, the dissolved sugar and yeast mixture, pinch of salt and the lemon zest. Knead thoroughly. Add more flour if necessary.

Divide the dough into 4 balls, cover and let rest for 30 minutes.

Heat the oven to 180°C (355°F). Butter and flour your baking tin. I used a 16×10 inch (40x25cm) pan.

On a floured surface roll out one part of the dough to the size of the baking tin, then lay it in.

Mix the ground walnuts (150g) with the powdered sugar (50g). Spread one third of the apricot jam on the first layer of dough. Sprinkle with third of the walnut-sugar mixture.

Roll out the second piece of dough. Put the jam on it and sprinkle with walnut-sugar mixture.

25

Roll out the third piece of dough. Spread the jam on it and sprinkle with walnut-sugar mixture.

Roll out the forth layer and place on top.

Bake the cake for 30 minute, until the top is light-brown. Let it cool completely.

For the chocolate cover: in a smaller pan melt 100 grams (3,5 ounces) butter, add 4 tablespoons of cocoa powder, 4 tablespoons of sugar and 4 tablespoons of water and stir until the sugar melts and the mixture thickens. Cover your cake with the chocolate sauce. The butter will make the chocolate have a glassy elegant look. Cut into diamonds and serve.

Havas Háztető

Ingredients (for 10):

1 kg of flour

300 grams of butter

100 grams of powdered sugar

40 grams of yeast

2 eggs

2 egg yolks

5 dl of milk

possible toppings: caster sugar, cinnamon, vanilla sugar, ground walnut, coconut flakes etc

Steps to Make It

Let the yeast rise in 1 dl lukewarm milk, and mix it with the flour, soft butter, powdered sugar, eggs and egg yolks. Add the remaining milk and knead the dough for 10-15 minutes. Let it sit in a warm place for an hour.

After the dough has doubled in size, roll it out and cut 1.5 centimetre wide strips. Wrap the strips around the buttered wooden dongs in a way that one layer slightly overlaps the next layer. Roll the dongs on the table so that the dough will be evenly spread. Then, roll the dough into the cinnamon sugar mixture (or whatever topping you chose to go for).

Some supermarkets carry wooden dongs, but if you can't seem to find any, wrap a smaller rolling pin with aluminium foil, brush it with butter and continue as if it was your homemade dong.

Place the wooden dong on a baking tin and bake your chimney cakes at 170-180° Celsius. Make sure to turn it two or three times until the sugar melts on the outside.

Enjoy the dessert!

Gesztenyepüré

Ingredients

31.75 ounces sweetened chestnut puree

4 tablespoons confectioners' sugar

1 tablespoon dark rum

1 cup heavy whipping cream

Optional: cocoa powder (to taste)

Garnish: long-stemmed maraschino cherries

Steps to Make It

Gather the ingredients.

In a medium bowl, mix together chestnut puree, confectioners' sugar, and rum. Place mixture into a ricer and portion out into serving dishes, swirling if possible.

Top with sweetened whipped cream, cocoa powder, and cherries, if using. Refrigerate any leftovers.

Aranygaluska

Ingredients:

For the dough:

350 g (~2 3/4 cups) flour

30 g (~2 tbsp) soft butter

200 ml (~little over 3/4 cup) lukewarm milk

2 tbsp sugar

20 g fresh yeast (2 tsp dry yeast)

2 egg yolks

zest of a half lemon

pinch of salt

For the topping:

100 g (~1/2 cup) butter, melted

100 g (~1 cup) ground walnuts

50 g sugar

For the custard:

800 ml (~3 1/3 cups) milk

4 egg yolks

seeds of a vanilla bean

3 tbsp sugar

2 tbsp flour

20 (~1 1/2 tbsp) ml rum

Steps to Make It

Dissolve yeast with sugar in lukewarm milk. Sift the flour in a bowl, add lemon zest , salt, egg yolks, butter and activated yeast, and with a mixer knead into an airy and very soft dough. Cover and in a warm place let it double in size (it takes about 40 minutes).

Butter a round cake pan; set a small bowl of water on the oven floor and preheat the oven to 180°C / 356°F. Turn out the dough onto a floured surface, roll out 2 cm (1 inch) thick and with a small cutter cut out balls. Reroll scraps and cut out more dumplings. To make the first layer, place balls into the prepared cake pan leaving some space between them (dumplings will rise during the baking process). Spread them with melted butter.

Combine ground walnuts and sugar, and scatter on top of the dough balls. Now comes the second layer of dumplings, brush melted butter on tops and sprinkle with ground walnut. (When the balls are prepared, I immediately slide them into the preheated oven; it's not necessary to let the dough rise for the second time, but you can leave it to rest if you want.) Bake for 35 minutes or until golden brown on the top.

For the custard combine egg yolks, sugar, flour, vanilla and rum, then add milk in small batches and whisk until lump-free and well combined. Over medium heat cook, while stirring constantly, until slightly thick.

Once the dumplings are done, serve warm, in "pull-apart" style, with the custard. This dessert is best out of the oven, but it will be still delicious when it cools to room temperature.

Somloi Galuska

Ingredients

1 Walnut Sponge Cake

1 Cocoa Sponge Cake

1 Plain Sponge Cake

Vanilla Pastry Cream

For the Rum Simple Syrup:

3/4 cup sugar

3/4 cup water

Optional: 1 (3-inch) strip orange zest

Optional: 1 (3-inch) strip lemon zest

Optional: 1/3 cup golden rum

For Assembly:

1/3 cup apricot preserves

1/2 cup walnuts (finely chopped)

1/2 cup raisins (golden or dark)

Garnish: 3 tablespoons cocoa powder (Dutch-processed)

For the Rum Chocolate Sauce:

3/4 cup water

Optional: 3 tablespoons golden rum

6 ounces chocolate (good-quality bittersweet, chopped)

3/4 cup sugar

For the Garnish:

Garnish: whipped cream (sweetened)

Steps to Make It

Prepare plain sponge cake, cocoa sponge cake, and walnut sponge cake per recipe instructions.

Prepare vanilla pastry cream per recipe instructions.

Meanwhile, make the Rum Simple Syrup by stirring the sugar, water, and orange and lemon zest, if using, in a small saucepan over medium heat until boiling. Continue to boil without stirring until the syrup has reduced slightly, about 5 minutes. Cool completely and stir in the rum, if using, and remove the zests, if using.

In a small saucepan, boil apricot preserves over medium heat and keep warm. Combine walnuts and raisins in a small bowl and set aside.

To assemble:

Place walnut sponge cake in the bottom of a 13x9-inch rectangular pan. Brush with 1/3 rum simple syrup, then spread with warm apricot preserves. Spread 1/3 pastry cream over the preserves and 1/2 the walnut-raisin mixture.

Next, place the cocoa sponge cake in the pan, pressing down lightly. Brush with 1/3 rum simple syrup and 1/3 pastry cream. Sprinkle remaining walnut-raisin mixture on top.

Top with plain sponge cake, pressing down lightly. Brush with remaining rum simple syrup and remaining 1/3 pastry cream. Sift 3 tablespoons cocoa powder over top. Cover with plastic wrap and refrigerate for at least 8 hours or overnight.

To make the Rum Chocolate Sauce: In a small saucepan over medium heat, bring 3/4 cup water, 3 tablespoons rum (if using), 6 ounces chopped chocolate and 3/4 cup sugar to a boil, stirring often. Reduce heat and cook at a brisk simmer, stirring often, until thickened, about 5 minutes. Cool slightly and serve warm.

To serve: The traditional presentation is to use a 2-inch ice cream scoop and place three "dumplings" in a bowl or on a dessert plate, then pipe with sweetened whipped cream and drizzle with the Rum Chocolate Sauce. A modern presentation is to cut the dessert into squares to show off the layers and then garnish with whipped cream and sauce.

Túrógombóc

Ingredients

500 grams of dry, crumbly cottage cheese (17.6 ounces)

2 eggs – separated

100 grams of semolina (or rice semolina) (3.5 ounces)

2 tablespoons of sugar

2 tablespoons of vanilla flavored sugar or 1 teaspoon of vanilla extract

Zest of a medium lemon

12 tablespoons of white breadcrumbs or ground walnuts

2 tablespoons of oil for toasting the breadcrumbs

Powdered sugar

Hungarian cottage cheese dumplings

Takes 30 minutes

Serves 14-16 medium sized balls.

Steps to Make It

Separate egg yolks from the whites. Beat the egg whites until stiff peaks form. Beat the egg yolks with two tablespoons of sugar and the vanillin sugar.

Place the cottage cheese in a bowl and crumble it or put it through a sieve. Add the egg yolk, the egg white, the semolina, and the lemon zest and stir to combine.

Put aside and let sit for 20 minutes, so the semolina absorbs moisture from the cheese. In the meantime, toast the breadcrumbs in oil over a low heat. Set aside.

Bring a large pot of lightly salted water to a gentle boil.

Shape the mixture into dumplings in the palms of your hands, moistened with water.

Slide the dumplings into the boiling water and stir gently for the first minute, to prevent sticking. Reduce the heat and simmer, uncovered, until the dumplings rise to the surface.

Remove the dumplings from the water using a spoon, drain and lightly roll them in breadcrumbs browned in oil.

Sprinkle with powdered sugar and serve with sour cream.

Túró Rudi

Ingredients:

For the sponge cake:

3 eggs

2 tbsp flour

1 tbsp cocoa powder

3 tbsp sugar

1 tsp baking powder

For the filling:

500 g (~1 lb) cottage cheese

200 g (~1 1/5 cups) powdered sugar

seeds of a vanilla bean

zest of a lemon

1 tbsp lemon juice

100 ml (~1/2 cup) sour cream

200 ml (~1 cup) whipping cream

1 1/2 tbsp gelatin

100 ml (~1/2 cup) water

For the glaze:

100 g (~3 1/2 oz) semi-sweet dark chocolate

1 tbsp oil

Steps to Make It

Line a 25 cm/10 inch springform round cake pan with parchment paper. Preheat the oven to 180°C / 356°F.

For the sponge cake combine flour, cocoa and baking powder. Separate the eggs, and whisk the egg whites until stiff peaks form. In a separate bowl beat egg yolks and sugar together to a ribbon stage. Stir the cocoa-flour mixture into the beaten egg yolks, then gently fold in the whipped egg whites. Pour the batter into the prepared cake pan and bake for about 15 minutes or until a toothpick comes out clean. Remove cake from the pan and let it cool on a wire rack.

Combine gelatin and water, and warm until gelatin dissolves completely (but don't boil it!). Set aside and cool until lukewarm. Place cottage cheese in a bowl. Add powdered sugar, vanilla, sour cream, lemon zest and juice, and mix until well combined. In a fine stream, while whisking constantly, pour gelatin into the mixture. Whip the cream until stiff, and gently fold into the cottage cheese cream.

Put the cocoa sponge cake in a clean springform round pan and spread the filling over the top evenly. Chill the cake for 3-4 hours.

Melt the chocolate over a pot of simmering water. Once it's fully melted, combine with one tablespoon of oil. Remove cake from the pan and pour the glaze over the top. Put the cake in the fridge until the glaze sets.

Máglyarakás

Ingredients:

For the sweet bread sticks:

200 g (~1 2/3 cup) flour

10 g fresh yeast (1 tsp dry yeast)

75 ml (~1/3 cup) milk

1 tbsp sugar

pinch of salt

1 egg

20 g (~1 1/2 tbsp) melted butter

For the custard:

600 ml (~2 1/2 cups) milk

seeds of a half vanilla bean

zest of a half lemon

4 egg yolks, 3 tbsp sugar

For the apple and apricot jam layer:

3 apples

1 tbsp sugar

50 g (~1/4 cup) butter

1 tsp ground cinnamon

5 tbsp apricot jam

1 tbsp rum

60 g (~1/3 cup) raisins

For the meringue:

4 egg whites

1 tbsp sugar

1 tbsp apricot jam

Steps to Make It

Dissolve yeast with sugar in lukewarm milk. Add egg, salt and activated yeast to the flour and start to knead. When the dough holds together, pour in melted butter and continue to knead until airy and pliable. Cover and let it double in size. On a floured surface roll out the dough into a 2 cm thick rectangle, and cut into 3 cm wide pieces. Place the sticks on a baking sheet lined with parchment paper and let them rise for 40 minutes. Preheat the oven to 200°C / 392°F and bake for 15-20 minutes or until golden brown. Let the sticks dry for a day.

Slice the sweet bread sticks and put into a large bowl. Soak the raisins in water.

Whisk egg yolks, sugar, vanilla and lemon zest together in a saucepan. Pour milk into the yolk mass in small batches to combine. Over medium heat cook, stirring constantly, until the custard becomes smooth and thickens a little. But don't bring it to a boil or the eggs will scramble. Pour over the stale pastry and stir to combine. Set aside to let it soak.

Peel and thinly slice the apples. Melt the butter in a frying pan, once it's hot enough, add apple slices, sprinkle with sugar and ground cinnamon, and cook until apple is almost tender.

Mix together 5 tablespoons of apricot jam and 1 tablespoon of rum, then warm it up a little in the microwave oven.

Preheat the oven to 180°C / 356°F. Grease an ovenproof rectangular dish, then dust with breadcrumbs. Lay the soaked sweet bread pieces in the prepared dish. Scatter the rinsed raisins over the top, then lay the apples on. Spread the warm rum apricot jam over the apple slices evenly. Place in the preheated oven for 20 minutes.

During the last 5 minutes prepare the meringue. Beat the egg whites with 1 tablespoon of sugar until soft peaks form, then beat in 1 tablespoon of apricot jam, and beat until very stiff. Remove the dish from the oven and spread the top with the whipped egg whites. Put the dish back in the oven and bake until top is light golden brown (for about 8-10 minutes). Let it cool to room temperature before slicing and serving.

Almás Rétes

Ingredients

For the Strudel Dough:

2 cups all-purpose flour

1 cup sour cream

1 teaspoon vinegar

1/4 teaspoon salt

2 large egg yolks (room temperature)

1 teaspoon baking powder

1 tablespoon butter (melted)

1/2 cup warm water

Melted vegetable shortening

1/2 cup bread crumbs

For the Apple Filling:

10 large Granny Smith apples (peeled, cored and thinly sliced)

2 cups sugar (or to taste)

1/2 teaspoon salt

8 ounces melted butter

Splash of lemon juice

Optional: 1 tablespoon cinnamon

Steps to Make It

Make the Strudel Dough

Gather the ingredients.

In a large bowl, blend flour, sour cream, vinegar, salt, egg yolks, baking powder, butter, and water. Knead for about 30 minutes. (The dough should be light and very smooth.)

Cover and let rest 1 hour.

Make the Apple Filling

Gather the ingredients.

Mix together thinly sliced apples, 2 cups sugar (or to taste), 1/2 teaspoon salt, 1 tablespoon optional cinnamon, 8 ounces melted room-temperature butter and a splash of lemon juice. Raisins and ground walnuts can be added, if desired.

Refrigerate, if not using immediately, but let it come to room temperature before filling the strudel dough. If a lot of juices have accumulated at the bottom, pour them off before placing on the strudel dough.

Assemble the Strudels

Cover a large table with a cloth and sprinkle it lightly with flour. Place dough in the center and roll it to about 1 inch thick.

Now flour your hands lightly. Place hands, palms down, under the dough and stretch gently in all directions toward the edge of the table. While stretching, ease dough by lifting it gently. Be gentle to prevent tears!

When stretched to the thinness of tissue paper, trim off the thick edges (this can be kneaded, rolled and cut into noodles). Spread dough with melted shortening. Let dough rest 10 minutes.

Sprinkle entire surface of dough with bread crumbs. Place apple filling all over the entire surface of the dough.

Preheat oven to 375 F. Use the cloth to roll the strudel away from you. Cut into two strudels. Tuck in the ends. Place on a parchment-lined baking sheet and brush the entire surface of strudel with melted butter.

Bake 30 minutes or until flakes start to separate and strudel is shiny and golden brown. Transfer to a wire rack to cool slightly. Cut into slices and serve slightly warm with ice cream or whipped cream.

Esterházy Torte

Ingredients

For the Sponge Cake:

5 large egg yolks

1 3/4 ounces sugar

1 3/4 ounces almonds (ground)

2 1/2 tablespoons all-purpose flour

3 large whites (stiffly beaten)

1/2 lemon (juiced)

Optional: 1 tablespoon vanilla

For the Chocolate Buttercream:

10 ounces chocolate (semisweet, chopped)

1 pound unsalted butter (softened)

5 large egg whites

1 cup sugar

For the Apricot Glaze:

1/4 cup apricot jam (melted and mixed with 1 tablespoon hot water)

For the Easy Fondant Icing:

3 cups powdered sugar

1/4 cup water

1 tablespoon light corn syrup

For the Garnish:

2 ounces chocolate (melted semisweet mixed with 1/4 teaspoon vegetable oil)

4 ounces sliced almonds (toasted or untoasted)

Steps to Make It

Heat oven to 350 F. Line four 8-inch round baking pans with parchment circles. Alternatively, you can line one 8-inch round pan with parchment, but you will have to split this cake into four layers.

Beat egg yolks with sugar until light and lemon colored. Sprinkle ground almonds and flour over batter and fold in gently. Fold in the egg whites and lemon juice or vanilla carefully so as not to deflate the batter.

Portion batter evenly into prepared pans. For four pans, bake about 10 to 15 minutes or until cakes pull away from sides of pan and top is golden brown. For one pan, bake 30 to 40 minutes or until golden. Cool in the pans.

Melt chocolate in a heatproof bowl in the microwave. Stir and set aside to cool. With a stand mixer or hand mixer, beat the butter with the paddle attachment on low for 2 minutes, medium for 3 minutes and high for 5 minutes. Transfer to a large bowl.

Place egg whites and sugar in the top of a double boiler over medium heat. Whisk gently to 120 F on a candy thermometer. Transfer to a clean and dry mixer bowl and beat with the balloon whisk on high until stiff peaks form; about 5 minutes. Fold melted chocolate into butter, then fold in egg whites.

On a serving platter, place one sponge cake layer and spread with 1/4 chocolate buttercream. Repeat 2 more times and top with the last sponge cake layer. Reserve the last 1/4 of buttercream for the sides. Refrigerate, covered, 1 hour.

Strain the apricot mixture and brush entire top of cake with glaze and let dry for 15 minutes.

Place all fondant ingredients in a small saucepan and stir until well mixed. Set over low heat and stir until dissolved. Don't let the temperature exceed 100 F on a candy thermometer. If glaze doesn't look opaque enough, add more powdered sugar.

Place chocolate-oil mixture in a squeeze bottle and set aside. Pour warm fondant over torte, tilting so the entire top is covered. If some drips down the sides, that's okay because it will be covered with the reserved buttercream. If it looks too transparent, you will have to apply another coat, but wait until this one dries.

If the fondant is the way you like it, before it dries, take the squeeze bottle and draw 4 or 5 concentric circles on the top of the torte. Using a skewer or the tip of a knife, drag it lightly through the lines from the center of the torte to the edge 8 times to make a chevron pattern.

Frost the sides of the torte with the reserved frosting, pressing in the sliced almonds. Refrigerate until ready to serve. For easier slicing, cut the torte while it is cold but let it come to room temperature before serving. This is a rich dessert, so small slices work best.

Raw Egg Warning

Consuming raw and lightly-cooked eggs poses a risk of food-borne illness.

Turos Lepeny

Ingredients

For the Crust:

2 1/2 cups all-purpose flour

1 cup confectioners' sugar

2 1/4 sticks butter, 1 large egg yolk

For the Filling:

1 pound dry curd farmers cheese (or ricotta)

1 cup sugar

3 large egg yolks

1 teaspoon vanilla

2 (14-ounce) cans apricot filling or jam

Optional: 1 teaspoon lemon zest

For the Meringue Topping:

4 large egg whites

1/2 teaspoon vanilla

1/2 cup sugar

Steps to Make It

Heat oven to 350 degrees. In the bowl of a food processor, mix flour and confectioners' sugar. Pulse in butter as for pie dough. Pour 1 egg yolk through the food chute and run the machine until dough starts to come together. Transfer the dough to a work surface and, lightly, bring the dough together. Press it into a 9x13-inch pan, using slightly dampened fingertips, if necessary. Bake halfway, about 20 minutes.

Meanwhile, in a large bowl or food processor, combine curd cheese, sugar, 3 egg yolks, 1 teaspoon vanilla, and zest (if using) until smooth. Note: If you like a lot of cheese filling, increase the curd cheese to 2 pounds, 6 large egg yolks, 2 teaspoons vanilla and 2 teaspoons lemon zest (if using).

Spread cheese filling evenly over partially baked crust, and top with apricot filling , using slightly dampened fingertips, if necessary, and return to oven for another 25 minutes.

Meanwhile, make the meringue by whipping the 4 reserved egg whites with 1/2 teaspoon vanilla and 1/2 cup sugar until stiff peaks form.

Reduce heat to 250 degrees. Remove cake from oven. Either pipe meringue over cheesecake surface in lattice-type rows or spread it evenly over the entire surface, using a spatula to make swirls as for lemon meringue pie. Bake 20 minutes or until meringue is very lightly brown. Cool completely before cutting into squares.

Sutemeny Rigo Jancsi

Ingredients

For the Sponge Cake:

3 ounces chocolate (unsweetened, melted, and cooled to lukewarm)

3/4 cup/1 1/2 sticks butter (unsalted, softened)

1/2 cup sugar (divided)

4 eggs (separated)

1 pinch salt

1/2 cup flour (all-purpose)

For the Filling:

1 1/2 cups heavy cream

10 ounces chocolate (semisweet, chopped)

4 tablespoons dark rum

1 teaspoon vanilla extract

For the Glaze:

7 ounces chocolate (semisweet, chopped)

2 tablespoons butter (unsalted)

2 tablespoons corn syrup (light)

1 teaspoon vanilla

Steps to Make It

To Make the Cake

Heat oven to 350 F. Line a jellyroll pan with parchment paper. In a large bowl, cream 3/4 cup butter with 1/4 cup sugar until light and fluffy. Add cooled melted chocolate and beat in egg yolks one at a time.

In a medium bowl, beat egg whites and pinch salt until whites cling to the beater. Add remaining 1/4 cup sugar and beat until stiff peaks form.

Lighten the chocolate mixture by stirring in 1/3 of the whites. Then, carefully, fold in the remaining whites. Sprinkle the flour over the batter and, carefully, fold it in without decreasing the volume.

Pour into prepared pan and bake 12 to 15 minutes, or until cake starts to pull away from the sides. Do not overbake. Cool a few minutes on a wire rack and then invert onto the rack. Remove parchment paper and let cool completely.

To Make the Filling

Meanwhile, place 10 ounces of chocolate in a heatproof bowl. Bring the cream to a boil in the microwave or on the stovetop and pour over chocolate.

Cover with plastic wrap and let stand 10 minutes. Add rum and vanilla and stir until smooth. Refrigerate 1 hour. When cold, whip the filling until the volume has doubled.

To Assemble the Cake

Cut the cake in half and place one half on a rack.

Spread the filling over the cake and top with the remaining cake half. Refrigerate for 1 hour.

To Make the Glaze

Meanwhile, place 7 ounces chocolate, butter and corn syrup in a microwaveable bowl. Heat on full power 1 minute. Add vanilla and stir until completely melted and smooth. Let cool 10 minutes.

Set the rack holding the cake over a pan to catch drips. Holding the glaze 2 inches above the cake, pour the glaze evenly, using a spatula to cover the sides, if necessary. Refrigerate 20 minutes or until glaze is set.

This cake is very rich. Cut into 5 by 7 rows for a total of 35 small squares. Refrigerate leftovers.

49971150R00042